HEINEMANN
Profiles

Richard
Branson

Rob Alcraft

Heinemann
LIBRARY

First published in Great Britain by
Heinemann Library
Halley Court, Jordan Hill, Oxford OX2 8EJ
a division of Reed Educational and
Professional Publishing Ltd.
Heinemann is a registered trademark of
Reed Educational & Professional Publishing
Limited.

OXFORD MELBOURNE
AUCKLAND KUALA LUMPUR
SINGAPORE IBADAN NAIROBI
KAMPALA JOHANNESBURG
GABORONE PORTSMOUTH NH
CHICAGO

Designed by Visual Image, Taunton.
Printed in Hong Kong / China

Details of written sources:
Mick Brown, *Richard Branson, The Inside
Story*, Michael Joseph, 1994; Tim Jackson,
*Virgin King. Inside Richard Branson's Business
Empire*, HarperCollins, 1994

02 01 00 99 98
10 9 8 7 6 5 4 3 2 1

ISBN 0 431 08622 2

**British Library Cataloguing in
Publication Data**

Alcraft, Rob, 1966–
   Richard Branson. – (Heinemann
   Profiles)
   1. Branson, Richard, 1950–
   2. Businessmen – Great Britain –
   Biography – Juvenile literature –
   3. Entrepreneurship – Great Britain –
   Juvenile literature
   I. Title
   338'.04'092[1]

Acknowledgements
The Publishers would like to thank the
following for permission to reproduce
photographs: Advertising Archives p47;
Camera Press: R Reid p18; Gamma pp5,
27, 30, 34, 46; Boccon Gibod p33; Heaven
nightclub p32 (top); Chris Honeywell p24;
KATZ Pictures p31; Mirror Syndication
International pp7 (both), 42, 44; Redferns
pp28, 32 (bottom); Sygma: G Pace p10, I
Vinomen p22, I Wyman p38; Time Inc: T
Spencer p19; Times Newspapers Ltd. p40;
Universal Pictorial Press & Agency pp4, 49,
50, 51, 53; Virgin pp6, 8, 9, 12, 26, 52.

Cover photograph reproduced with
permission of Universal Pictorial Press and
Agency Ltd.

Every effort has been made to contact
copyright holders of any material
reproduced in this book. Any omissions will
be rectified in subsequent printings if notice
is given to the Publisher.

Any words appearing in the text in bold,
like this, are explained in the Glossary.

19

CONTENTS

WHO IS RICHARD BRANSON? 4

BORN LUCKY 6

BEGINNING IN BUSINESS 12

THE BIRTH OF VIRGIN 16

RISKY MONEY 20

MAKING RECORDS 24

A VIRGIN ISLAND 30

FLYING HIGH 34

BALLOONS AND BUSINESS 38

'YOU CAN DO PRETTY WELL
ANYTHING' 46

RICHARD BRANSON – THE VIEWS 50

RICHARD BRANSON – TIMELINE 54

GLOSSARY 55

INDEX 56

WHO IS RICHARD BRANSON?

Richard Branson is a millionaire businessman. He is a record-breaking balloonist, an adventurer and a practical joker. He is also a walking advertisement for his growing Virgin business empire. The company he started from nothing is now worth about £1.6 billion.

His Virgin business sells records, holidays, wedding dresses, cosmetics, soft drinks, and runs nightclubs, a bank, an investment company and – the thing Branson loves most – an airline.

Richard Branson, the UK's best known businessman.

He has a reputation as a daredevil and risk-taker. Richard Branson says he has come close to death 11 times. He was the first to cross the Atlantic and Pacific Oceans in a hot-air balloon. He narrowly escaped death attempting to fly round the world in a balloon. He was within 90 seconds of crashing into the ground.

He is impatient, persuasive and a man who wants to win. Yet he also wants to help. He headed a **campaign** to give jobs to the young unemployed, called UK2000. He began a young people's advice

Strange publicity stunts are Branson's trademark.

service nearly 30 years ago, and still pays its running costs. In 1987 he launched a new low-price condom called Mates, to help prevent the spread of Aids.

Branson has got where he is by motivating people and by making deals. The deals almost always work out in his favour. 'If you ask Branson to lend you £5,' says one business partner, 'he will knock you down to £4.50.'

> 'My general philosophy is, if you decide to do something, throw yourself into it, and do it well, and enjoy it as much as you can.'
>
> Branson, *The Times*, 1996

BORN LUCKY

Richard Branson was born on 18 July 1950. His father, Ted, was training to be a barrister. His mother, Eve, helped add to their small family income by embroidering cushions in a shed at the bottom of the garden. She says her son 'was an absolute handful. And he has been a handful ever since'.

A DIFFERENT SORT OF FAMILY

Richard Branson's family has always been a little out of the ordinary. His grandmother is in the *Guinness Book of Records* for getting a hole-in-one in a game of golf. She was aged 90. His uncle was an eccentric known for eating home-dried hay. His mother worked for one of the first airlines. She was used to crash-landing in a desert.

Branson's childhood was happy.

Eve wanted the same sort of bravery and sense of adventure from her son when he was a child, but she thought he was getting soft. So, at four years old, Richard Branson found himself in a Devon field near his grandparents' house. His mother told him, as a challenge, to find his own way back to the house.

Branson, aged two, at his grandparents' farm in Sussex.

Branson's childhood dream was to become an explorer.

It was dark before Branson wandered to the door of a nearby farmhouse and rang the bell. He got a lift home and proved that whatever else he was, he was lucky.

EXPLORING AND DOING

As a child Branson decided he wanted to become an explorer. He had the fields and woods around his parents' Sussex home as his playground. He spent most of the time either breaking something or hurting himself.

'I think I was lucky. I had very loving parents and was brought up in the countryside in a cottage and I had a lot of freedom to roam.'
Branson, 1997

Branson was expected to be independent and confident. Branson says that his mother 'wouldn't let us watch football, we had to be playing football. She wouldn't let us go and watch a film, we had to create a film. Her whole thing was that you must be *doing* all the time.' This need to be always doing something has stayed with Branson.

SCHOOL DAYS

At the age of eight, Branson was sent to boarding school near Windsor. He hated it and did not do well. 'I was slightly **dyslexic**,' he says ,'and I was getting behind in my work. I think I spent most of my time playing sport.' Branson was good at sport, and he was captain of just about every team in the school. But even this had to stop after one football match put him in hospital with a seriously injured knee.

His parents lost hope that he would pass any exams. 'I once did an **IQ test**,' says Branson. 'I remember sitting there looking at this piece of paper and I suspect I scored less than anyone in the history of IQ tests! It just didn't make sense to me *at all*.' But in the end the exams didn't matter. At 14 years old Branson was offered a place at a **public school** called Stowe. They would take him on

Branson, bottom left, was good at sport.

the strength of his interview alone. He was already an expert at talking himself into anything – a skill that was to make him rich.

At Stowe School Branson was soon failing exams again. 'I suppose I was rebelling against school,' he says, 'rebelling against a lot of things I didn't like.' Outside school the world was changing rapidly. It was the 1960s. It was the decade of rock 'n' roll and **hippies**. Young people were breaking all the rules about what they should do, and how they should behave. Branson wanted to get out into the world and *do* something.

When Branson was 16 he wrote to his father saying he had had enough of school and wanted to leave. His father at first insisted he needed to stay at school and get qualifications. But then Ted remembered how he had been pushed into being a barrister by his own father. He visited Branson the next weekend, and told his son he was free to leave.

INTO THE WORLD

'Branson, I predict you will either go to prison, or become a millionaire,' were the headmaster's words as Branson left Stowe School in 1967. His parents said he could not come home. If he insisted on leaving school then he would have to support himself. No-one seemed quite sure what Branson was going to do with himself. Like his headmaster, they feared he could go either way.

Branson with his mother and father. They taught him to believe in himself.

Branson threw himself into his new life. Before he had left Stowe School he had begun work on a new magazine, to be called *Student*. He had persuaded most of the sixth form to write letters begging for contributions from the rich and famous. Now he and a group of friends, including his childhood friend Nik Powell, moved into a dark London basement. They did not have to pay rent because it belonged to a friend's mother. This small dark space was their home and the office for the new magazine. Branson was going to launch his business on the world. He felt his magazine was a good idea and was determined to make it work.

Trees and budgerigars

Before *Student* magazine, Branson's business experience was limited to Christmas trees and budgerigars. One school holiday, years before, he had calculated that tree seedlings cost a few pence, but Christmas trees sold at £1 a foot. If he grew enough trees he could be up to £600 in profit. He and his friend Nik Powell cleared a patch of land in a corner of his parents' rambling garden. But the two boys lost interest in the project and a population of rabbits finished the trees off.

Breeding and selling budgerigars also started as a promising idea. But Branson was always looking for new excitement and forgot about them, leaving the selling to his father.

BEGINNING IN BUSINESS

'Hello, I'm Richard Branson, I'm 18 and I run a magazine that's doing something really useful for young people.' Branson was on the phone. He had a low, confident **public school** voice, and was trying to persuade yet another famous person to write for his magazine. *Student* magazine had not even been published yet, but Branson was unstoppable. He had confidence and sometimes just cheek, and would call or write to anyone. He usually got a result. If he didn't, he would move on to the next call.

Even in the chaos of his basement offices, Branson had a gift for convincing people that he was worth taking notice of.

PRINTING PROBLEMS

But one day he had a call himself. It was a firm of printers. He had persuaded them to give him three months' credit. They would print the magazine, and he could pay them later with the money he made from selling it.

But the printers had just found out that, because he was so young, he would not be legally responsible for any **debts**. The printers were nervous and told him they were pulling out of the deal.

Branson took advice from his father. There was a meeting between the printers, teenage Branson and their lawyers. Luckily a contract had been signed. The printers had little choice but to print the magazine as promised. *Student* magazine was saved, at least for now.

MONEY

In the early days Branson was dogged by money problems. He simply never had any. He was forced to develop sly habits. When people turned up at the ramshackle offices, expecting to be paid, he wouldn't be there. Getting money out of him took skill. His friends gave up asking Branson for money. They forged his signature on cheques and paid themselves their wages.

The list of famous writers who contributed to *Student* grew. There were articles about ideas and politics. What people wrote about did not matter too much to Branson, as long as they did it for free.

ALBION STREET

In 1968 Branson and his friends were told to move from their dark basement. The general dirt and

'He just wouldn't go away. He was one of those people who it was just easier to do what he asked, and get rid of him; otherwise he'd be on your doorstep every five minutes, driving you mad.'

Ian Howes, *Town* magazine

chaos were too much for his friend's parents. So they moved to a house in Albion Street, London, that was rented by Branson's parents. This quickly became just as chaotic and dirty.

Albion Street had a constant stream of visitors. People came to take away bundles of magazines to sell on the streets; others came to help write it, produce it, and design it; others came just for somewhere to stay. Life was adventurous and fun. Although there was still no money, life in the house seemed like a constant party.

FREE ADVICE FOR STUDENTS

It wasn't always easy for Branson. When his girlfriend became pregnant they faced many problems. Their difficulties made such a deep impression on Branson that he started the Student Advisory Centre. It gave young people advice on any problem, from sex to depression.

The service was free and still runs today. He began it because he wanted to help. Soon, desperate young people were joining the stream of visitors to Albion Street.

Journalists also visited the house. They wrote stories for newspapers about the busy office with its constant telephone calls and visitors. Little did they know that Branson would send a friend to a phone box round the corner and get them to make calls to the office until the journalists had left. Even at the age of 18 Branson knew the value of good publicity.

GETTING STARTED

It was Branson's energy that kept *Student* and Albion Street going. No-one else was interested in finding advertisers and paying bills. 'I became a businessman only because I wanted to be an editor and put the magazine out,' says Branson. 'I had to make the magazine pay for itself, and survive.'

But it was becoming difficult to avoid the awful truth. Piles of magazines sat in corners unsold. From those that were sold, very little of the money ever got back to Branson – the people who sold them often walked off with the money. Branson fell ill from the pressure of running the magazine, and it finally collapsed in 1969. He needed a better money-making scheme, and he needed it quickly.

THE BIRTH OF VIRGIN

It was 1969 when Branson told his friends at Albion Street about his new scheme. He would sell records through the post at discount prices.

It was a good idea. Record companies had been keeping the price of records high for years. Lots of people would want to buy records at Branson's cheap prices. The friends talked about what to call the new **mail-order** business. Someone suggested Slipped Disc. Branson suggested Virgin – because business was new to them. The name stuck.

RECORDS

The first advertisement for the Virgin mail-order business appeared in the music **press**. Along with the bills and final demands, the morning post brought orders from all over Britain. Branson bought the records in bulk, sold them cheaply, and still made a **profit**.

Branson knew little about the music he was selling so he asked friends who did know about it to work for him. Working with Branson was fun. 'It was like being in a gang with Richard as the leader,' said one of his friends. Branson knew the value of friends. He wanted Nik Powell, his childhood friend, to help him run the business. To persuade him Branson offered him a 40 per cent share of Virgin.

STRIKE

In 1970 the economy of Britain hit trouble. Unemployment was rising and it cost more and more to live. The postal workers voted to go on strike. The streams of record orders and cheques in the morning post disappeared. Branson suddenly had no business.

OPENING UP SHOP

Now that Branson could not rely on the mail-order business he decided to open a record shop. This opened in 1971 in Oxford Street, London. It was tucked away up some steps and very scruffy. But on the first day there was a queue stretching all the way round the street corner. Word had got round about the new, cheap record shop.

The shop prided itself on selling only 'cool' music. **Hippies** could sink into old armchairs to listen to serious rock music. Sometimes they would still be there at the end of the day, not having bought a record.

'The one secret of our success is people. If you can find the right people, look after those people, motivate those people, you can achieve pretty well anything.'

Branson, 1997

Branson's record shops found a ready market with young people. They wanted good music but at cheap prices.

Business at the record shop seemed good and Branson soon opened another shop in Liverpool.

RECORDING STUDIO

Branson had often talked with his friends about the business empire he was going to build. One of his plans was to own his own record label. It meant he had to set up a recording studio, sign artists, and **compete** with the giant record companies.

Some of his friends were a little worried. Everything Branson did was a bit risky. His business always seemed one deal away from collapse. Branson himself never seemed to have doubts. With the shops now running well, he bought £800 worth of recording equipment, borrowed money from an aunt, and bought Shipton Manor in Oxfordshire as a home and recording studio.

His girlfriend at the time, speaking to one of Branson's **biographers**, remembers Branson showing her round and, before the contracts were even signed, she said he was whacking bricks out of a fireplace saying, 'We'll have that open.' It was typical Branson, he was one step ahead of even himself. He was, as always, looking for the next project and the next bit of excitement.

Branson relaxes at Shipton Manor. He bought the Manor as a home and recording studio at 21 years old.

£60,000 IN DEBT

Richard Branson was 21. He had two record shops, a **mail-order** business and a manor house. But he had borrowed a lot of money to buy them. He was £60,000 in **debt**. His accountant told him that the only option was to sell everything.

'Branson could make the most unlikely things happen ... . This sense that anything was possible, and nothing would stand in his way.'

Chris Strangeways,
who worked with Branson in the early days

RISKY MONEY

Branson always seemed in control. But he knew he needed money to keep his business going. By accident he discovered a way to avoid tax on record sales and make the money he needed. It worked like this. If you sold records abroad you could claim tax back from the government. All you needed were some documents that were stamped when you left the country with the records.

Branson was eager to have a go. He bought a load of very cheap, very bad records and drove them to Belgium. There, he dumped them on a tip. It was the documents that had been stamped that were valuable. He used these to claim back tax he had never actually paid. One trip made him £8000 better off. Unfortunately, it was illegal.

But Branson needed the money too much to stop. Soon he was not even bothering to dump old records abroad. He just drove up to the port with an empty van, picked up his valuable and illegal documents, drove round the port for a while, and then went straight home.

ARRESTED

On the evening of 28 May 1971, Branson's mother, Eve, got a telephone call. It was Branson and he was in tears. He had been arrested by Customs and Excise. He appeared in court the next morning. His mother put up £30,000 **bail** – the value of the family house – to keep him out of prison.

But Branson found that the Customs and Excise office did not want him in jail, they wanted his money: £15,000 now, and £38,000 over the next three years. He wasn't in prison, but he was more broke than ever.

> 'A night spent in the cells with just a filthy blanket and one drink and you learn never to do it again.'
>
> Branson

EXPANDING OUT OF TROUBLE

Branson and his old friend Nik Powell decided they had two choices. They could either sell out and pay the debts, so that Branson could avoid prison. Or they could take a risk and try to expand out of trouble, by opening more shops.

It was beautifully simple, if a little risky. They worked out that they could get four weeks' **credit** if they opened a new shop at the beginning of a month. This was because the companies which sold them records were willing to give them up to 30 days to pay. The more shops they had, the more cash

The first Virgin record shops were scruffy and small. Today shops like this Virgin Megastore are big money earners for Branson.

would flow through the business. It would look good and they could carry on borrowing from the bank. Hopefully they would eventually make a **profit**.

Branson and Powell opened a third Virgin record shop in west London, and another in Brighton. For the next two years they opened a new shop every two months.

TILL RAIDING

The cash did begin to flow but Branson had little idea about accounting. He would frequently raid the tills of the Virgin shops. When the shop manager came to count the cash at the end of the day, he would find, along with a few coins, a crumpled IOU from Branson. In the end Nik Powell had to tell all the shops not to let Branson take their money – unless he gave them a cheque first.

A FREE LUNCH

Branson's attitude to much of his business was just as chaotic. He had a million pound **turnover** and employed 40 people, but he could not read a **balance sheet**. One day he took his bank manager out to lunch at an expensive restaurant. Branson did not have a tie on, so the restaurant would not let him in. After he borrowed one and got in, the restaurant then refused his cheque at the end of the meal. His bank manager had to pay instead!

MAKING RECORDS

I t was May 1973 and, as in the old days of *Student* magazine, Branson was making a nuisance of himself on the phone. He was calling radio stations across the country trying to get them to play Virgin's new record. It was difficult because the record was unusual. Instead of a collection of songs, it was several long instrumentals.

The record was called *Tubular Bells*. A musician called Mike Oldfield had spent nine months recording the album at Shipton Manor in Oxfordshire. He played every single instrument on it himself, and there were more than 20.

Tubular Bells, the record that made Branson his first £1 million.

THE DEAL

The usual way for a small record company like Virgin to release a record was to sell it on to another label in return for a small part of the **profits**. If the record failed, then they lost little. Branson wanted a better deal. If this record succeeded, he wanted Virgin to get the money. He eventually persuaded a bigger company to press the record, and let him do the **marketing** and **advertising**. Virgin would get most of the profits if the record was a success. If it failed, Virgin would be broke.

Tubular Bells was released in May 1973, along with three other albums. These were the first releases on the new Virgin label. A disc jockey, called John Peel, played the entire *Tubular Bells* album on Radio One. It gave the album the credibility it needed and money poured in from sales.

WORK CAN BE FUN

In the early days of the record company it was Branson's sense of fun that kept people loyal. He was always playing practical jokes, taking people out for meals, and giving parties. His staff worked for less money than they could get elsewhere – some even turned down jobs with double the pay. They enjoyed working for Branson.

Not everyone liked it though. One employee who left said that working for Branson was like being in a religious cult. For others the endless round of parties and dinners and weekends away made work fun.

Love and marriage

Just as Virgin's first records were beginning to sell, Branson married Kristen Tomassi on 22 July 1972. She had come to Britain from America for a two-week holiday, and Branson had only just persuaded her to stay – by kidnapping her suitcases!

Branson and Tomassi were married at a church in Oxfordshire near Shipton Manor. As ever, with his eye on business, Branson had his bank manager as a particularly special guest at the wedding.

But the constant work put a strain on Branson's marriage to Tomassi. After two years she left, feeling she would always come second to the business.

Branson and Kristen Tomassi, enjoying their wedding day in 1972.

Branson is always willing to join in the fun.

MAKING IT BIG

The money from *Tubular Bells* allowed Virgin to build its business. It signed a string of new bands. Branson was constantly thinking big. The big names could bring **profits**, and the sort of reputation that would attract good new pop bands. In 1975 Branson came close to signing 10cc, and then the Rolling Stones – at a price of $4 million. But the deals fell through at the last minute.

Then, one day, when Branson was watching television, he saw an interview with four drunken and threatening youths called the Sex Pistols. The interview consisted mainly of swearing. The nation was outraged, but young people loved it. Branson was interested. He thought he saw his next record signing, his next challenge.

'If the people who run a company enjoy life, and they're smiling and they're happy and not taking themselves too seriously, then it's much easier for all the people within the company to do the same.'

Branson, 1997

Johnny Rotten of the Sex Pistols. Outrageous and loud, the band made money for Virgin.

ON A BOAT WITH THE SEX PISTOLS

Branson stood on the bridge of a pleasure boat called the *Elizabethan*. It was the week of celebrations for the Queen's Silver Jubilee in 1977, and the boat was heading for Parliament along the Thames. With Branson on the boat were the four frightening youths he had seen on television: the Sex Pistols. Branson had signed them to Virgin, but not before two other record labels had actually *paid* them to leave.

The reputation of **Punk**, and the Sex Pistols, went before them. Two police launches closed in on the pleasure boat. Then, as they neared the Parliament building on the Thames, the Sex Pistols began a screaming version of *God Save the Queen*. Shouting through loud-hailers the police launches drew alongside and were soon boarding the *Elizabethan*, forcing it in to shore. Chaos broke out as the Sex Pistols were wrestled off the boat into waiting police vans. Branson tried to quieten things down and managed to avoid being arrested.

PUBLICITY

'To have one lone voice attacking royalty in Jubilee week seemed perfectly fair,' said Branson. 'It also happened to sell a lot of records, and was great for the company.'

His parents didn't think it was so great. Like many older people in Britain, they were disgusted by the Sex Pistols and made their disapproval perfectly clear to Branson. But for the Virgin label the Sex Pistols' behaviour was excellent publicity.

A Virgin Island

In 1978, with the money coming in from *Tubular Bells* and the Sex Pistols, Branson began what seemed like a series of crazy schemes. One involved flying to Jamaica to sign up new bands. He took a suitcase stuffed full of money with him.

A few weeks later Branson was back in the Caribbean. He wanted to buy a Caribbean Island. He did not have nearly enough money, but found that the seller was desperate for money. He was asking $4.5 million; Branson got the island for $300,000 making another profitable addition to his empire.

Richard and Joan with their two children.

Family

In 1976 Branson met Joan Templeman, who had come to Shipton Manor in Oxfordshire with a friend. Richard and Joan fell in love and lived together for 12 years. They married in 1989, joking that they thought they should get married before their two children did.

Joan has kept herself, and their children, firmly out of the public eye. But their friends say that Joan and his family have kept Branson's feet on the ground through years of success and celebrity. 'We've managed to keep our personal lives out of the **press**,' says Branson.

See-saw

Branson bought Necker Island in the Caribbean for a knock down price.

Virgin's fortunes see-sawed through the early 1980s. Losses of £900,000 in 1981 became a **profit** of £1.5 million by the next year. Branson expanded the Virgin business into other areas. He bought two nightclubs, a part share of a hotel, and even began selling computer games.

Party time at Branson's Heaven nightclub.

BUSINESS BOOMS

In 1983 Virgin struck lucky again. An artist called Boy George, an outrageously dressed singer and songwriter, signed up with Virgin. By the time his fourth single was released he was one of the biggest stars in the world. Virgin's **turnover** rocketed to £94 million, with **profits** of £11.4 million. Branson now had an empire of over 40 companies, including cinemas, clubs, restaurants and films. Branson was 33 years old.

Boy George became a worldwide star and made Virgin millions of pounds.

Much of Branson's life is taken up at big meetings.

Nearly all Branson's new companies started from nothing. His style, as in the days of *Student* and the **mail-order** business, was to motivate people who knew more about the products to run the businesses. 'What we do is appoint really good people to run each company,' says Branson. 'We give them a personal stake in each of the companies, and let them run them as though they were their own ... I spend most of my time with new ventures.'

'He is tremendously persuasive. He can convince all sorts of people, from Boy George to city investors, that it might be a good idea to tag along. Once you start tagging along you start doing your extra hour here, your extra hour there... . Much of it is to the benefit of Richard in reality, but for some reason you feel quite happy doing it. It is partly a fact of life never being dull.'
Don Cruikshank, Virgin's Managing Director

FLYING HIGH

Branson's next business venture was his most risky yet. It was an airline – Virgin Atlantic. A businessman approached him with the idea and asked Branson to put up the money. It was a high cost, high risk project. A few big companies controlled most of the profitable **air routes** around the world. They could, and would, try to squeeze any competition out of the market.

Branson got a route from the UK to America, and a licence to fly from Britain's Civil Aviation Authority. Next he needed an aeroplane. He struck a very complex deal with Boeing, a company that built aircraft. The deal meant the Virgin company would survive, even if the airline didn't.

'I hated flying with other people's airlines – I had a passion to put it right. There was not one redeeming factor about them that was pleasant. The staff didn't smile, the food was terrible, there was no entertainment, they were unclean … they were just like transporting cattle.'

Branson, 1997

FIRE ON BOARD

Now there was just the hurdle of a first inspection flight. It seemed a formality. Branson flew by helicopter to Gatwick Airport, outside London, to pick up the plane. There it stood, just four months after the idea had first been put to Branson, bright and splendid in new Virgin colours.

But as the plane climbed from take-off there was a loud bang. From the windows Branson and the aircraft inspector could see flames shooting from one engine. On the ground Branson found that repairs would cost £600,000. But worse than that a journalist had it all on film. There could easily be another inspection flight, but with a story of a fire in the newspapers, there would probably be no airline. But Branson's luck seemed to hold. The cameraman, friendly and smiling, destroyed the film.

'When we actually got into the airline business people said we were absolutely mad, everyone else who tried to get into the airline business had failed.'

Branson, 1997

On 22 June 1984 Virgin Atlantic made its first flight to the USA. Branson's new business passion had begun. From the start he was obsessed with the airline. He loved the detail and the negotiating. Built from nothing, he felt the airline was entirely his.

FLYING TOO HIGH?

Branson soon found that the airline business was not going to be an easy ride. **British Airways** slashed its prices. Other airlines followed. They were trying to **undercut** Branson, because they couldn't afford to lose passengers to a new airline. Branson needed to advertise to **compete** with the big companies.

SINKING BOATS

'I decided to use myself to **promote** my company,' says Branson. Now the adventures really began. In 1985 Branson attempted to break the record for the fastest boat crossing of the Atlantic, from America to the UK. The high-powered boat was called *Challenger*. It pounded through the waves for more than two days before smashing into floating debris off the south coast of Britain. It was only hours away from the record. Branson and the crew had to abandon ship. It was dangerous, exciting and plucky. It became Branson's trademark, and it made good business sense. One newspaper estimated the failed attempt to cross the Atlantic had earned £50 million in free **advertising** for Virgin. Bookings on Branson's airline increased almost immediately.

The right image

Using himself to promote Virgin at that time worked for Branson because he was likeable. He was not slick and arrogant like many businessmen. His halting speech, and 'umming and aring' seemed endearing. If journalists wanted to question him they could phone and, most of the time, they could actually get to talk to him. People thought of him as 'one of us'.

PASSENGER TICKET AND BAGGAGE CHECK
SUBJECT TO CONDITIONS OF CONTRACT

ISSUED BY virgin atlantic

NAME OF PASSENGER (NOT TRANSFERABLE)
TEST/MR
LONDON/HEATHROW   VS..1   J 23MAR1600.OK
O NEWARK

ORIGINAL ISSUE   ISSUED IN EXCHANGE FOR
FARE CALCULATION
/FC LON VS NYC2677.87JW VS LON2508.06JX NUC5185.93END ROE0.58890SITI
XT3.00YC1.20XA14.40USXF1.80EWR3

FARE
GBP 3054.00
GB 20.00
TAX   XY 3.60
        XT 20.40
TOTAL
GBP 3098.00   93201015265042   1 932 2120277028 2

DATE OF ISSUE   FLIGHT COUPON 1 OF 2
ISB. AGT. ID   18MAR98 91494723 SITI GB
        A66026AM   /LONDON

PASSENGER TICKET AND BAGGAGE CHECK
PASSENGER COUPON
BOARDING PASS   8
NAME OF PASSENGER
TEST/MR
FROM
LONDON/HEATHROW
O NEWARK
VIRGIN ATLANTIC AIRW
CARRIER/FLIGHT CLASS/DATE TIME
VS 1   J 23MAR1600.
CHECK IN REQUIRED

1 932 2120277028 2

virgin atlantic

virgin atlantic

'DIRTY TRICKS'

A ticket from Branson's airline, which has survived fierce competition and dirty tricks.

Competition for passengers was fierce. Bad rumours and stories began to spread about Virgin Atlantic. A rival airline, British Airways, had launched what became known as a 'dirty tricks **campaign**'. They wanted to put Branson's airline out of business, whatever it took. They offered Virgin passengers cheaper flights or even free flights if they flew with British Airways.

COUNTER ATTACK

In the 1990s when competition for airline passengers was greater than ever, Branson launched a public counter-attack on British Airways. He accused them of trying to put him out of business and spreading lies about the Virgin company. In 1993 he took them to court to prove his case. 'We won the court case against British Airways,' says Branson. 'That was a turning point. Before, there were lots of questions about our finances. By winning, people like Boeing were willing to do business with us.'

'He [Branson] is a sort of Robin Hood on the side of the punter against the robber barons seeking to rip them off.'
Financial Times,
1 November 1997

BALLOONS AND BUSINESS

Keeping Virgin Atlantic Airways going had become a battle that Branson was determined to win. He busily **promoted** himself and the airline at any and every opportunity. With a boat called *Challenger II* he succeeded in breaking the transatlantic record set in 1952. Then in 1987 he crossed the Atlantic in a hot-air balloon. It was the first time it had ever been done.

CROSSING THE PACIFIC

In 1990 Branson attempted to cross the Pacific Ocean, thousands of miles of open sea, in a balloon. 'I think this was the longest and most terrifying moment of my life,' says Branson. 'We dropped this empty fuel tank, but somehow there had been a short in the electrical wiring. Half the fuel tanks went with it, so we'd lost about eight or nine tonnes of fuel.'

'We did our calculations and realised that the only way that we could cross the Pacific was by averaging 265 kph in the balloon. It just was not possible for a balloon to go that fast. There was a force nine gale blowing and there were no ships below, because it was so rough. We had to accept the fact that the chances of us coming home were very unlikely.'

SPEEDING IN A BALLOON

Branson and his co-pilot, Per Lindstrand, survived. They managed to get the balloon up into the jet stream, a fast current of air high above the earth, where their speed climbed to 322 kph and then 354 kph.

Ready for lift off. Branson attempts the first ever balloon crossing of the Pacific Ocean. They stayed awake for 50 hours. 'In a situation like that the key is not to give up, and to fight as best as you can,' says Branson. In the end they made it across the Pacific Ocean. It was a triumph.

WAR

In Britain, Branson's 'near death' over the Pacific Ocean hardly made the news. While he was in the air, a war had started in the Middle East. The USA and Britain were involved.

The war began a spiral of **recession** in the airline business. Oil went up in price. The number of passengers fell. In 1991 this forced Branson to sell the Virgin Music Group – the record company – to a rival company called Thorn-EMI. Virgin's music business was Branson's first and most profitable company. He got £560 million from the sale. Few people guessed how much Virgin needed the money.

DISAPPOINTMENT

But Branson is not always lucky. One photograph that appeared in many British newspapers was of Branson with his head slumped in his hands. He looked the very picture of disappointment. Branson had lost the bid to run the National Lottery. His scheme was to run it as a **charity** and not to take

In 1998 Branson's lottery disappointments were forgotten. Branson proved in court that rivals had offered him bribes not to bid for the lottery. He proved his honesty, and was awarded £100,000.

THE TIMES 35p

No. 66,115 — TUESDAY FEBRUARY 3 1998 — http://www.the-times.co.uk

THE COST OF FREE LOVE
Libby Purves
PAGE 18

HODDLE'S CHOICE
England call-up for 18-year-old
PAGE 52

GUSCOTT'S RETURN
Lions' rugby hero back for Five Nations
PAGE 46

THE GIFT OF HOPE
How Times readers may save Dorah's sight
PAGE 16

UNDER THE SKIN OF SPORT

Defeated lottery chief resigns

£100,000 libel case victory for Branson

By Joanna Bale and Jon Ashworth

Surrounded by his wife and family, Richard Branson emerges from the High Court after winning £100,000 libel damages and costs. His wife, Joan, is beside him on the left

profit from it. He saw it as the only honest way to handle such a **monopoly**. Those in the British Government who decided who should run the Lottery, thought differently.

It was typical Branson – thinking big – not trying to win the lottery, but trying to *run* it. 'Success in my opinion is trying,' says Branson. 'If you try something, and if you fail, you've actually succeeded more than someone who doesn't try things... .
It took me 25 years before I felt that our company was safe from going **bankrupt**, the whole 25 years of many occasions where the banks nearly closed us down.'

BIG BALLOON ADVENTURE

In 1997 Branson attempted another great balloon record. He would fly round the world. It was exciting and it was good publicity. It was also dangerous. 'I love challenging myself with things like the boating trips, and the ballooning trips,' says Branson. 'And trying to see if we can achieve things which people say are impossible.'

THE *VIRGIN CHALLENGER*

Branson's new balloon, the *Virgin Challenger*, was to fly to 9,144 metres, and hitch a ride with the jet stream – the fast current of air high up above the earth that had taken him across the Pacific Ocean at 354 kph.

Ready for lift-off again – Branson and his team prepare for a round-the-world flight.

They would launch from Marrakech in Morocco, where the weather was usually good. A crew of more than 150 people flew to an airbase outside Marrakech to get everything ready for the launch.

Race against time

On the morning of Monday 6 January 1997, the sun rose over a clear blue sky. The huge silver balloon was laid out over the tarmac of the Moroccan airbase. By 8 pm the operation to pump in helium – a gas lighter than air – had begun. Over the coming hours the balloon began to take shape. Its great silver bag towered 61 metres into the air. But would it carry Branson round the world?

Ninety seconds from death

By late afternoon on 7 January, the balloon had crossed the Atlas mountains in north Africa. But by nightfall something was seriously wrong. The balloon began to fall. At 610 metres a minute it was falling faster than an express lift. In a few minutes the crew knew that the balloon would smash into the desert, and they would be dead. Here are the next minutes from Branson's diary.

'Per [one of the three pilots] shouts: "Dump everything." Seven minutes to go. Helium is spilling out. Something is terribly wrong. I throw out food, water supplies, anything I can lay my hands on. Oil cans next. Our supplies are gone. The dream is over. I just want to live.'

As the balloon hurtles earthwards, Alex, one of the crew members, has to climb out on to the capsule roof to try and release the one-tonne fuel tanks.

'Per shouts: "Get back inside. We've got 90 seconds left." We throw ourselves back into our seats. We are still hurtling down. There are only seconds left

The Virgin Challenger. It brought Branson and his team close to death.

before we smash into the ground. Alex and I shout: "Can we parachute?" It's too late. The capsule can withstand a fall at 305 metres a minute. We are falling at 610 metres a minute. Per throws the **explosive bolt** with 610 metres left.

One tank drops away. We soar into the air. What a wonderful feeling.'

DESERT LANDING

Twelve hours later Branson and the crew brought the balloon into land, bumping gently into the Algerian desert. Branson says, 'I remember thinking "If we ever get out of this alive, I will never do it again." Three hours later when we were sitting in the spectacular Sahara, I was not so sure.'

Branson is always resilient, willing to try. In a typical act, when Branson dumped everything from the balloon, he kept two bottles of champagne. For Branson there is always something to celebrate. When the crisis is over, it is time to start again.

'I enjoy life, but I want to try again. I want to do it. I am 99 per cent certain we are going back.'

Branson, *The Times*, 10 January 1997

'YOU CAN DO PRETTY WELL ANYTHING'

'**P**ersonal experience is the best way of tackling business,' says Branson. 'I have never read a business book. We do things and then work out afterwards what the strategy was.'

Looking at business in this way has worked for Virgin, which is now an empire with sales of £1.6 billion. 'We start with one shop or one plane,' says Branson, 'and then try to create something special. And if people like it, we try to build it up from there. I think the mistake people make is if they ask, "How can I make a lot of money?" If you start from that way round you're very unlikely to make a lot of money.'

Branson chats to a member of staff aboard a Virgin aircraft.

'If you have a really happy group of people working for you,' says Branson, 'you can do pretty well anything.'

For Branson himself, money doesn't appear to matter that much. It is just a way to make things happen; to start new businesses; to plan new adventures.

His new companies include everything from trains to pensions and even a bank. He works long hours, but work for Branson *is* fun. One minute he will be trying to strike a deal with a room full of business people – the next he will be messing around in an open air bath to promote a new company.

The Virgin business now includes everything from insurance to make-up. Branson is the man behind it all.

DOES THE INSURANCE INDUSTRY HAVE CAUSE TO FEAR THIS MAN?

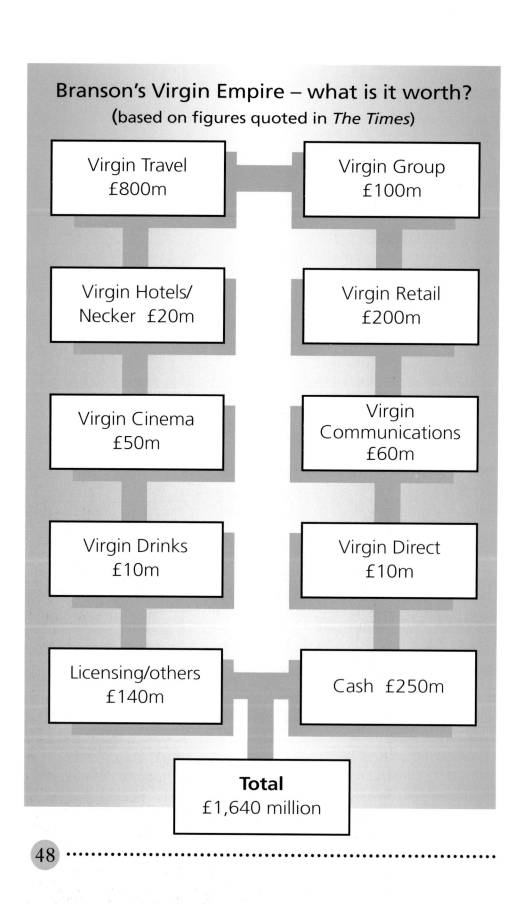

Branson's Virgin Empire – what is it worth?
(based on figures quoted in *The Times*)

Virgin Travel £800m

Virgin Group £100m

Virgin Hotels/ Necker £20m

Virgin Retail £200m

Virgin Cinema £50m

Virgin Communications £60m

Virgin Drinks £10m

Virgin Direct £10m

Licensing/others £140m

Cash £250m

Total £1,640 million

In January 1998 Branson's latest round-the-world balloon attempt failed. The balloon broke free of its mooring and crashed, without Branson and the crew. Yet the attempt still got Branson the publicity he wanted. Talking to him, you get the feeling that it will always be like this; whatever happens he will come up smiling: in some way he will have won.

Branson with Pamela Anderson. His public image is relaxed and fun, but he is a serious and powerful businessman.

Richard Branson – The Views

'He was not at all clever,' said Branson's old school headmaster in 1992. But Branson has never let people's thoughts dent his confidence. He was clever, but not in the way he was supposed to be.

He has made himself the face of the Virgin empire. He has cultivated an image of someone who is slightly unorthodox, daredevil and fun to be with. The idea is that we think the same of Virgin products, and go out and buy them.

'I decided to use myself to **promote** my company,' says Branson. 'If by turning up in a captain's outfit to promote our airline it gave the photographers a better picture, then I'd turn up in a captain's outfit. I'd feel kind of goofy sometimes, but if it got on the front pages of the newspapers across the world ... that's £5 million of **advertising**.'

"I feel a bit goofy sometimes ... ' Branson says, as he uses himself to promote Virgin.

Not everyone believes in Branson's pleasant image. A journalist who once worked for him said, 'Branson doesn't know what the rules are. He'll see something and go for it, and not worry too much about the obstacles. Sometimes these obstacles may be people.'

Most people agree that Branson is as he seems. In fact it is hard to find bad things written or said about him. For a man who is so successful and so much in the public eye, you would expect him to get more criticism than he does.

Never afraid to act the fool, Branson plays up to the camera at the launch of another business, Virgin Bride.

'In his own charmingly haphazard way, Branson runs the slickest Public Relations machine in Britain.'   *Sunday Times*, 1993

'He is a man in a hurry, used to command and action: anyone who takes him as laid-back is clearly making a big mistake.'
Daily Telegraph, 1 May 1997

Mr Nice

Branson is the most well-known businessman in Britain, and the most popular, according to a 1996 survey in the *Sunday Times* newspaper. But when you talk to Branson, he assumes nothing. He does not assume you know about his business, or about him. He is polite and after just a few minutes you can see why people enjoy working for him.

Branson's first office and home was a houseboat.

Even cynical journalists have all been taken by his charm. 'Branson is a beguiling man,' says one journalist from the *Sunday Telegraph* newspaper, 'quieter and more **elusive** than his public image suggests. He seems wholly without arrogance. He rarely talks about Virgin except as *we*.'

Branson has charm and he has gone out of his way to get involved with things that matter. He launched Mates condoms to help stop the spread of Aids. He still funds the Student Advice Centre, now called Help, that he set up for young people in the 1960s. There are also stories of operations paid for, parties arranged, and favours done.

WINNING WAYS

Some people have confused Branson's pleasant unassuming manner and charm with weakness. They have underestimated him. Lord King, the chairman of **British Airways** during the 'dirty tricks **campaign**' did so. He is reported to have said that if only Branson had worn a suit and shaved off his beard, he would have taken him more seriously. Branson did neither, and when British Airways lost their court case to Branson, it cost Lord King his job.

Branson is well known and well liked.

'Every day I get hundreds of letters and hundreds of telephone calls, and I know I let most of these people down. Fifteen years ago [before he was well known] I could have responded to everyone properly.'

'I'm still very nervous when I go on TV, or give public interviews. It's fairly unnatural, sitting talking to millions of people.'
Branson

Above all, Branson wants to win. His energy and impatience are as well known as his charm. 'Richard is always building an empire, even when he is standing at the bus stop,' says a former business partner. 'He'll probably incorporate three or four people into the company before the bus comes.'

RICHARD BRANSON – TIMELINE

1950 Richard Branson born

1956 Begins primary school

1964 Starts at Stowe School, Buckinghamshire

1966 Begins *Student* magazine

1967 Leaves Stowe School and moves to London to produce *Student* magazine

1968 First edition of *Student* magazine. Begins Student Advisory Centre.

1969 Starts **mail-order** record company

1970 Gives childhood friend Nik Powell 40 per cent of Virgin company

1971 Post strike; opens first Virgin record shop
Buys Shipton Manor in Oxfordshire and sets up recording studio
Arrested by Customs and Excise

1972 Marries Kristen Tomassi

1973 *Tubular Bells* makes Branson a millionaire

1976 Meets and falls in love with Joan Templeman

1977 Signs Sex Pistols to Virgin label

1978 Buys island in the Caribbean

1981 Launches *Event* magazine; magazine fails.

1982 Pop artist, Boy George, signs with Virgin

1984 First flight of Virgin Atlantic Airlines

1985 Adventures begin. First attempt on Atlantic crossing record fails

1987 Crosses Atlantic in hot-air balloon
Launches new condom called Mates

1989 Marries Joan Templeman

1990 Flies Pacific Ocean in hot-air balloon

1992 Sells Virgin Music Group to Thorn-EMI for £560 million; needs money

1993 Court action against **British Airways** is settled; Branson wins

1994 A bid for Britain's National Lottery is unsuccessful

1997 Attempts round-the-world flight in hot-air balloon; crash-lands in north African desert

1998 Second round-the-world balloon attempt fails

GLOSSARY

advertising a way of telling people about what you make or do, and getting them to buy it, such as through TV advertisements

air route like an invisible corridor in the sky. Only a limited number are allowed so aircraft do not crash into each other

bail a sum of money demanded by a judge in court. If paid it allows an accused person to go free until their trial

balance sheet a list of all money made and owed by a company

bankrupt when a business can not pay its bills, and has to close

biographer someone who writes the life story of a person

British Airways the UK's largest airline company

campaign trying to change the law or make something happen

charity an organization such as Comic Relief or Oxfam

compete take part to try and win

credit buying something, and not having to pay until later

debt owing someone money

dyslexic someone who finds it difficult to read or count because words and figures seem jumbled up

elusive hard to find, or hard to understand

explosive bolt a bolt that is made to come undone quickly

hippie followers of a 1960s fashion for long hair, flared trousers and a peaceful outlook on life

IQ test stands for 'intelligence quotient'. The test is supposed to measure how clever someone is

mail-order a business that has no shops but works through the post

marketing a plan for selling products

monopoly a business that has no competitors

press another name for newspapers and magazines

profit the money a company has left after paying all its bills

promote to make sure lots of people know lots of good things about you or your business

public school a school where parents pay for pupils to attend

Punk a 1970s fashion in music and lifestyle. It was loud and rude and about rebelling against authority

recession a bad time in a country or business when there is little money or another serious problem

turnover the total money which a company earns, before it pays its bills

undercut selling something for less than someone else – with the idea of taking their business away

INDEX

Boy George 32
Branson, Eve and Ted 6, 8, 10, 21
Branson, Richard
 arrest 21
 business style 5, 17, 27, 33, 46
 character and image 4, 36, 50, 51, 52, 53
 childhood 6–7
 death, escapes from 4, 39, 45
 dyslexia 8
 early business experience 11
 marriages and children 26, 30, 31
 popularity 52
 schooldays 8–10
British Airways 36, 37, 53
Challenger 36, 38
Customs and Excise 21
'dirty tricks campaign' 37, 53
Help (Student Advisory Centre) 4–5, 14–15, 52
hot-air ballooning 4, 38–39, 41–45, 47
King, Lord 53
Lindstrand, Per 39, 43, 44, 45
mail-order record business 16–17
Mates condoms 5, 52
money problems 13, 19, 21, 31, 40

National Lottery 40–41
Necker Island 30, 31
Oldfield, Mike 24
Peel, John 25
Powell, Nik 11, 16, 22, 23
promotion and publicity stunts 5, 15, 36, 38, 50, 51
Punk 29
record company 18, 24, 25, 27, 32, 40
record shops 17–18, 22–23
Sex Pistols 27–29, 30
Shipton Manor 18, 19, 24
Student 11, 12–13, 15
Templeman, Joan 30, 31
Tomassi, Kirsten 26
transatlantic boat crossings 36, 38
Tubular Bells 24, 25, 27, 30
UK2000 4
Virgin
 businesses 4, 31, 32, 47
 company value 4, 48
 employees 25–26, 33, 47
 turnover and profits 31, 32, 46
Virgin Atlantic Airways 34–35, 36, 37, 38
Virgin Bride 51
Virgin Challenger 41, 44